MW01088732

Noah Webster's Reading Handbook

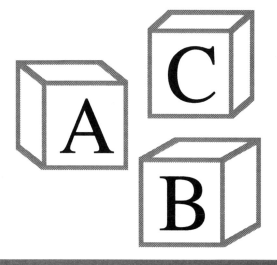

-- Written by --
Darrel A. Trulson

Copyright © 1993 Christian Liberty Press
2005 Printing

All rights reserved. No part of this book may be reproduced
in any form or by any means, except for brief quotations
for the purpose of review, comment, or scholarship, without
written permission from the publisher.

Christian Liberty Press
502 West Euclid Avenue
Arlington Heights, Illinois 60004
www.christianlibertypress.com

ISBN 1-930092-24-5

Printed in the United States of America

Preface

Noah Webster is still highly regarded in educational circles even though he has been dead for over one hundred and fifty years. His reputation has survived the test of time because he played a key role in laying the foundation for standardized word meanings and pronunciation in the English language when the United States was a very young nation.

Webster was the first American to produce an authoritative and comprehensive dictionary for the people of the United States. His first dictionary was completed and printed in 1828. Although Webster's dictionary brought him long lasting notoriety and fame, this was not his only significant publication.

Several years before his dictionary was in print, Webster produced a practical book that was used in the school houses of America to teach primary reading, phonics and spelling. This book, known as *The American Spelling Book* or popularly referred to as *The Blue-Backed Speller*, was an instant success and endured as the standard reading text in America for over a century. In fact, the printing royalties from this reading handbook helped to sustain Webster financially during those years in which he was preoccupied with working on his now famous dictionary. Millions of copies of *The Blue-Backed Speller*, along with books like the Bible and the McGuffey's readers, gave young people in America an excellent foundation in the areas of reading, phonics and spelling.

The book that follows, *Noah Webster's Reading Handbook*, is an updated and modernized version of the old *Blue-Backed Speller*. It may be used in any grade to teach the fundamentals of phonics and reading, or as remedial work for older students.

We are confident that this book will carry on the tradition of providing students with an excellent foundation in reading, spelling, and Biblical values.

Michael J. McHugh
Curriculum Director

Introduction

This Handbook is very simple to use. First of all, the alphabet charts at the beginning of the book should be repeated every day until the student has them memorized. Please note that it is not as important to teach the names of the letters, as it is to teach the sounds which they make.

After your student has the letters and their principle sounds memorized, you can move into the rest of the book. We recommend that you spend as much time as necessary on each page, especially in the beginning, as you instruct the student on the various letters, blends, words and sentences. Do not move onto a new page, until your student can sound out all the letters and words on the current page.

To sound out a blend or word, pronounce the first letter or blend and then add the final letter or blend ("**tr**" -- "**ail**" -- "**trail**"). Emphasize each sound separately and then tie them together. Teach the concept to your student that vowels and consonant go together to form blends, and the blends are the building blocks of all the words we use.

Eventually, sentences are presented in the lessons to teach how the words are connected together to express ideas and thoughts. Have your student sound out all the words in the sentences. Then, after having learned the words, encourage them to read the sentences more quickly. Try skipping back to sentences learned in prior lessons, so that the student does not simply memorize the sentence being taught, but is actually reading the words by way of decoding the sounds.

The charts in the back of the Handbook are to be taught

during the course of your instruction. Refer to the bottom of the lesson page to see which chart to use. These charts are effective for review purposes and to help the student who is having difficulty in understanding a particular blend.

It is a good idea to regularly go through the lessons and review prior sections with your student. Important principles taught one day can be easily forgotten a week or so later.

If resources permit, purchase a set of flash cards to help in the memorization of the vowels and consonants. As your student begins reading, write the common or troublesome words onto index or recipe cards. Review these daily until your student can say them without hesitation. This will offer you variety in your teaching style and help your student to assimilate what he has learned more quickly.

It is recommended that you spend no more than twenty minutes at a time on each lesson or subject. A younger student with a short attention span will benefit more from two or three short periods than one long lesson.

You may discover that a student will have difficulty grasping certain concepts. If this occurs, simply take a break from the subject for a few days and then come back to it fresh. This time away from the subject is sometimes needed for conceptualization to completely occur before moving on to new material.

Finally, begin and end each reading session with prayer and thanksgiving for the opportunity the Lord has provided each of us to learn how to read. Reading is a precious gift and one which your student will value the rest of his life.

The Alphabet

Memorize the alphabet, learning both the letters and the sounds they represent. Drill the sounds of the vowels and consonants daily until they are mastered.

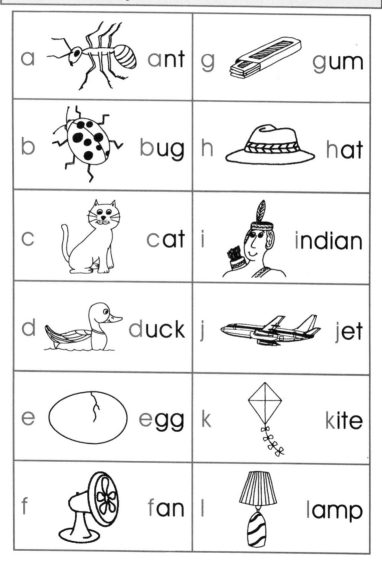

a	ant	g	gum
b	bug	h	hat
c	cat	i	indian
d	duck	j	jet
e	egg	k	kite
f	fan	l	lamp

Chart 1　1

The Alphabet

m	mop	t	turtle
n	nest	u	umpire
o	ostrich	v	van
p	pin	w	walrus
qu	quilt	x (ks)	box
r	ring	y	yarn
s	seal	z	zebra

The Short Vowels

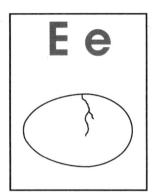

ă ĕ ĭ ŏ ŭ

Chart 1 **3**

The Long Vowels

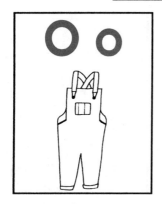

ā ē ī ō ū

The Consonants

B b	K k	S s
C c	L l	T t
D d	M m	V v
F f	N n	W w
G g	P p	X x
H h	Q q	Y y
J j	R r	Z z

Chart 1   5

A a

ant

As the following words are read, listen for the a-ant sound.

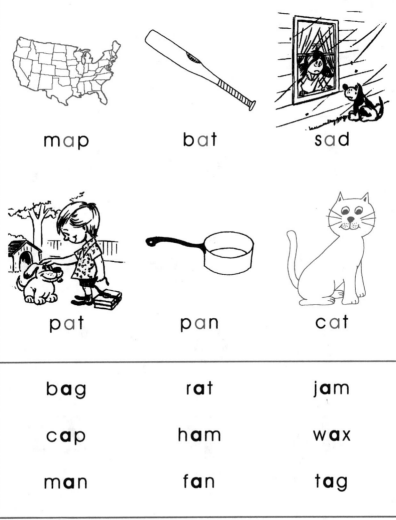

map	bat	sad
pat	pan	cat

bag	rat	jam
cap	ham	wax
man	fan	tag

E e

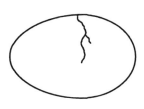

egg

As the following words are read, listen for the e-egg sound.

net

well

tent

pen

hen

wet

men	gem	pet
sell	den	bell
jet	vet	egg

Chart 2   7

I i

Indian

As the following words are read, listen for the I-Indian sound.

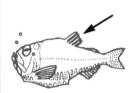

fin

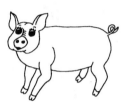

pig

mix

mitt

fist

sing

hill	sit	it
fix	lid	is
sip	hit	in

O o

ostrich

As the following words are read, listen for the o-ostrich sound.

| hop | stop | rod |
| fox | rock | clock |

top	pop	cot
sob	ox	mop
pot	dot	doll

Chart 2   9

U u umpire

As the following words are read, listen for the u-umpire sound.

bud   run   tub

sub   cuff   drum

nut	hug	rug
bus	suds	cup
pup	up	tug

Short Vowel Review

Listen for the short vowel sound as you say each of these words.

ă	ĕ	ĭ	ŏ	ŭ
apple	egg	Indian	otter	under
ant	engine	igloo	ox	umpire
ax	elbow	ink	olive	up

map	ten	pig	Rob	tub
man	net	fit	top	nut
hat	jet	lid	doll	hum
had	Deb	did	rod	rut
bat	well	wit	log	gum

sad	leg	bus	van
cut	cub	till	tap
sob	ten	ham	fig
fuss	sit	men	Todd
dots	run	Bob	bun

Chart 2 **11**

S s  seal

Look at the vowel and say the sound. Add the consonant and say the blend. Complete the exercise and read the word.

ă	ĕ	ĭ	ŏ	ŭ
s a	s e	s i	s o	s u
s i	s o	s a	s u	s e
s ap	s et	s ip	s od	s ub

s a	s u	s e	s o
s i	s o	s i	s a

sun	six	sit	sad
sub	sell	sod	sap

Rule: When a word has only one vowel and it comes at the beginning or between two consonants, the vowel is usually short.

T t

turkey

Look at the vowel and say the sound. Add the consonant and say the blend. Complete the exercise and read the word.

ă	ĕ	ĭ	ŏ	ŭ
ta	te	ti	to	tu
ti	to	ta	tu	te
tap	ten	tip	top	tug

ta	te	ta	to	te
tu	ti	ti	te	to
to	tu	tu	ti	ta

Ted	top	till	tab	tub
ten	tell	tot	tan	tag
sap	set	sub	sod	sip

Chart 3   13

B b

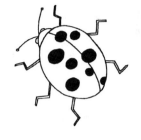

bug

Look at the vowel and say the sound. Add the consonant and say the blend. Complete the exercise and read the word.

ă	ĕ	ĭ	ŏ	ŭ
ba	be	bi	bo	bu
bo	ba	bi	be	bu
bag	bell	big	box	bud

be	bu	bu	bi	be
ba	bo	bo	ba	bi
bi	be	ba	bu	bo

bat	beg	bus	log	bit
top	tug	tot	tag	tell
sad	sip	sit	six	sock

H h

hat

Look at the vowel and say the sound. Add the consonant and say the blend. Complete the exercise and read the word.

ă	ĕ	ĭ	ŏ	ŭ
ha	he	hi	ho	hu
ho	ha	he	hi	hu
hat	hen	hip	hop	hum

ha	he	hi	hu	ha
hi	hu	ha	ho	he
ho	he	ho	hi	hu

hen	hill	had	hut	hog
bet	box	bat	Bill	bug
tax	tan	top	tug	Tim

Chart 4   15

F f

fan

Look at the vowel and say the sound. Add the consonant and say the blend. Complete the exercise and read the word.

ă	ĕ	ĭ	ŏ	ŭ
fa	fe	fi	fo	fu
fi	fa	fe	fu	fo
fact	fret	fig	fog	fun

fe	fi	fo	fe	fu
fo	fa	fi	fu	fa

hat	hem	hub	hop	hit
bib	Bob	bug	bat	bed
tab	tug	tell	tip	Tom
sob	suds	sad	sin	set
egg	it	as	up	in

M m

mop

Look at the vowel and say the sound. Add the consonant and say the blend. Complete the exercise and read the word.

ă	ĕ	ĭ	ŏ	ŭ
ma	me	mi	mo	mu
mo	me	mi	ma	mu
mat	met	mill	mom	mug

mo	mi	mu	ma	mi
mu	ma	mo	me	me

fix	fed	fun	fan	fox
hum	had	hit	hot	hen

Important words which help to connect sentences are: **a, the, and, to, I,** and **into.** Please learn to use these words.

Chart 4   **17**

C c   K k

cat   kite

Look at the vowel and say the sound. Add the consonant and say the blend. Complete the exercise and read the word.

ă	ĕ	ĭ	ŏ	ŭ
c a	k e	k i	c o	c u
k i	c o	c a	c u	k e
c at	K en	k id	c ot	c up

c a	c o	k i	c a	k e
c u	k e	c u	k i	c o

a	the	and	to	into
m e ss	m o p	m a p	m u d	m itt

Rule: The letters **c** and **k** share the work of the k sound. The **c** works with the vowels a, o and u. The **k** works with the vowels e and i.

D d

dart

Look at the vowel and say the sound. Add the consonant and say the blend. Complete the exercise and read the word.

ă	ĕ	ĭ	ŏ	ŭ
da	de	di	do	du
di	do	da	du	de
dad	den	dip	dot	dug

da	de	di	do	du
do	di	du	de	da

can	kiss	cod	Ken	cud
mug	mill	map	mob	met
the	into	I	and	a
fell	fit	fat	fun	fox
ham	hop	hill	hen	hum

Chart 5 **19**

J j

jet

Look at the vowels and practice saying the consonant blends. Read the words and the sentences until you know them.

ă	ĕ	ĭ	ŏ	ŭ
ja	je	ji	jo	ju
ji	jo	ja	ju	je
jam	jet	Jill	job	jug

dot	did	dug	den	dam
cop	Ken	cat	kid	cuff
a	the	and	to	I
met	mom	map	mud	mix
fun	fat	fit	fog	fed

Bill fed the hen.

Jill had a pet pig.

R r

ring

Look at the vowels and practice saying the consonant blends. Read the words and the sentences until you know them.

ă	ĕ	ĭ	ŏ	ŭ
ra	re	ri	ro	ru
ri	ro	ra	ru	re
rat	red	rib	rob	rug

jet	jam	jug	Jim	jog
at	is	in	as	it
bud	bet	big	bad	box
ten	tag	tug	Tim	top
sad	sod	sell	sin	sub

Deb had a hat.

The cat is fun.

Chart 6   21

G g

gum

Look at the vowels and practice saying the consonant blends. Read the words and the sentences until you know them.

ă	ĕ	ĭ	ŏ	ŭ
ga	ge	gi	go	gu
ga	gu	go	gi	ge
gag	get	gill	got	gun

rag	red	rub	rid	rod
Jed	jam	jug	Jill	jog
dad	Deb	dill	dug	dot
Ken	cup	call	con	kid
met	mop	mug	mix	mad

Jill got a doll.

Is Deb mad?

L l

lamp

Look at the vowels and practice saying the consonant blends. Read the words and the sentences until you know them.

ă	ĕ	ĭ	ŏ	ŭ
la	le	li	lo	lu
le	lu	li	la	lo
lap	let	lick	log	luck

bag	mat	led	lip	top
tag	fat	fed	tip	mop
rag	sat	bed	rip	cop
gag	bat	Ted	dip	hop
lag	hat	red	sip	pop

Jed is a cat.

The bug is in the jam.

Chart 6   23

N n

nest

Look at the vowel and say the sound. Add the consonant and say the blend. Complete the exercise and read the word.

ă	ĕ	ĭ	ŏ	ŭ
na	ne	ni	no	nu
nu	no	ni	ne	na
nag	net	nip	not	nut

lock	luck	lid	let	lab
God	get	gas	gum	gill
rob	rub	red	rat	rib
at	is	it	on	up
dad	dell	did	duck	dot

Here are more important sight words which help build sentences: **come, what, do,** and **two**. Please learn to use these words.

W w

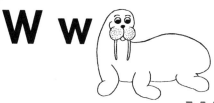

walrus

Look at the vowels and practice saying the consonant blends. Read the words and the sentences until you know them.

ă	ĕ	ĭ	ŏ	ŭ
wa	we	wi	wo	wu
wu	wo	wa	we	wi

bell	tack	kill	tug	not
well	sack	fill	bug	pot
fell	back	mill	mug	hot
tell	jack	hill	hug	lot
sell	rack	Bill	jug	cot

Can I get a job?

The duck has a tub.

Ted has a red bed.

Chart 7   **25**

P p

pin

Look at the vowels and practice saying the consonant blends. Read the words and the sentences until you know them.

ă	ĕ	ĭ	ŏ	ŭ
pa	pe	pi	po	pu
pa	pu	pi	po	pe
pat	pen	pig	pot	puff

wag	wet	wow	wig	well
net	nut	nap	nick	nod
leg	list	lass	luck	log
get	God	gag	gun	gill

Tom hit the peg.

26   Chart 7

V v

van

Look at the vowels and practice saying the consonant blends. Read the words and the sentences until you know them.

ă	ĕ	ĭ	ŏ	ŭ
va	ve	vi	vo	vu
ve	vo	vu	va	vi

puff	pad	pod	pin	peg
wok	win	wag	wick	web
nod	nut	nest	nab	nip
less	log	luck	lip	lap
two	do	what	come	into

Bill fell into the mud.

Hop up the hill.

Can I sell the cat?

Chart 8 **27**

Qu qu

quilt

Look at the vowels and practice saying the consonant blends. Read the words and the sentences until you know them.

ă	ĕ	ĭ	ŏ
qua	que	qui	quo
quo	qui	qua	que

vim	Vick	vat	vet	vest
pop	pen	pit	pup	pat
wet	will	wow	wag	wax

Ken has a big hen.

The red can is hot.

The **Q - q** always has the vowel **u** next to it. They make the same sound as **kw**. How **qu**ickly can you learn this sound?

Y y

yarn

Look at the vowels and practice saying the consonant blends. Read the words and the sentences until you know them.

ă	ĕ	ĭ	ŏ	ŭ
ya	ye	yi	yo	yu
yi	yu	ye	ya	yi

pot	pig	gum	quack	pen
hot	dig	hum	back	den
tot	fig	sum	sack	ten
not	big	bum	tack	Ben
lot	wig	yum	rack	hen

Ben will get the duck.

Chart 8   **29**

X x

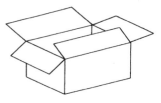

box

Look at the vowels and practice saying the consonant blends. Read the words and the sentences until you know them.

ă	ĕ	ĭ	ŏ	ŭ
ax	ex	ix	ox	ux
ux	ox	ax	ex	ix
tax	next	fix	fox	tux

yam	yum	yes	yell	yet
quack	quill	quit	quest	quiz
vat	vet	van	vest	vim
Peg	pin	pad	puff	pot
do	was	the	what	come

The **X - x** sound is made by saying the consonants **k** and **s**. The **X - x** is usually at the end of words.

Z z

zebra

Look at the vowels and practice saying the consonant blends. Read the words and the sentences until you know them.

ă	ĕ	ĭ	ŏ	ŭ
za	ze	zi	zo	zu
zu	zo	za	ze	zi
Zac	zest	zip	zot	Zug

him	but	had	met	sod
Tim	rut	mad	set	rod
dim	cut	sad	yet	God
Jim	hut	bad	let	nod

Tim went up

to Deb.

Chart 9 **31**

A a

acorn

Listen for the long vowel sound as you say each of these words.

a̅y	a̅_e	a̅i
da	ca	pa
day	cake	paid

ray	fake	laid	day	lake
pay	take	nail	Fay	bake
bay	vane	bait	hay	ape
say	gate	pail	lay	tame
may	wave	raid	pay	game

Rule: When there are two vowels in a word, the first vowel says its long sound, and the second vowel is silent.

These are the vowel blends which make up the long **A - a** sound: **a**, **ai**, **a_e**, and **ay**. Look and listen to the long **A - a** vowels.

E e

eagle

Listen for the long vowel sound as you say each of these words. Review the short vowel words.

ēa	ēe	ēy
bе	sе	kе
bead	seed	key

heel	leaf	sheep	beak	bee
tree	teach	deer	bead	Jeep
keen	seat	keep	meal	eel
feet	peas	weep	read	Lee
queen	heat	sleep	seal	deep

map	wet	pig	rod	bug
pat	leg	lid	doll	but

These are the vowel blends which make up the long **E - e** sound: **e**, **ea**, **ee**, and **ey**. Look and listen to the long **E - a** vowels.

Chart 10 **33**

I i

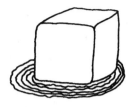

ice

Listen for the long vowel sound as you say each of these words. Review the short vowel words.

ī_e	ȳ	īe
ti	fli	pi
tide	fly	pie

time	pie	fly	site	try
pine	tie	sky	bite	sly
wise	die	dry	tire	by
hive	lie	cry	tide	my
bite	tie	fry	size	pry

hat	hen	wig	sod	tug
bad	pet	bib	rob	sub

These are the vowel blends which make up the long **I - i** sound: **i, i_e, ie** and **y**. Look and listen to the long **I - i** vowels.

O o   overalls

Listen for the long vowel sound as you say each of these words. Review the short vowel words.

ōe	ōa	ō_e	ōw
ho	so	ro	cro
hoe	soap	rope	crow

bow	bone	goat	rope	toe
row	home	toast	cone	doe
bowl	nose	coal	pole	foe
tow	note	toad	yoke	hoe
slow	hope	soap	rose	poem

vat	net	Jim	dot	mug
cab	fed	mix	not	fun

These are the vowel blends which make up the long **O - o** sound: **o, oe, oa, o_e** and **ow**. Look and listen to the long **O - o** vowels.

Chart 10 **35**

U u

uniform

Listen for the long vowel sound as you say each of these words. Review the short vowel words.

ūi	ū_e	ew
su	cu	fu
suit	cute	few

cube	suit	pew	tune	drew
tube	juice	stew	fuse	blew
mule	fruit	new	rule	flew

gas	hem	Jill	cot	puff
pass	pen	fit	log	dug

Don't forget, when there are two vowels in a word, the first vowel says its long sound, and the second vowel is silent.

These are the vowel blends which make up the long **U** - **u** sound: **u, ui, u_e,** and **ew**. Look and listen to the long **U** - **u** vowels.

Long Vowel Review

Listen for the short and long vowel sound as you say each of these words.

bā	kē	dī	tō	fū
bake	keat	dive	toad	fruit
bait	keep	die	tow	few
bay	key	dry	toll	fume

hid – hide	van – vane	tub – tube
bat – bait	bed – bead	pin – pine
rod – road	hop – hope	wet – wheat
mad – made	cub – cube	sop – soap
kit – kite	pan – pain	cut – cute

Sue reads the poem.

Jake takes a rest.

Chart 10 **37**

bl

block

Carefully watch the long and short vowels as you read the blends, words and sentences.

blā	blē	blī	blō	blū
blă	blĕ	blĭ	blŏ	blŭ

cube	juice	pew	fuse	tube
row	home	toast	cone	doe
time	tie	fly	bite	sly
heel	teach	deer	beak	bee
pay	fake	laid	Fay	lake

My pup is black.

His name is Jed.

Jed is a big black pup.

Do you remember the short vowel rule? When a word has only one vowel and it comes at the beginning or between two consonants, the vowel is usually short.

cl

clock

Carefully watch the long and short vowels as you read the blends, words and sentences.

clā	clē	clī	clō	clū
clă	clĕ	clĭ	clŏ	clŭ

class	close	clay	clip	clod
club	clap	clot	claim	clash
clam	clue	clean	click	cluck

bluff	bled	blob	black	blow
blast	blame	bless	bleed	blip
bleak	bliss	blaze	block	blade

Can Jill see the time on the clock?

We best get into bed.

The long **A** - **a** vowel blends are: **a**, **ai**, **a_e** and **ay**. Practice saying these with the different consonants and blends.

Chart 11 **39**

fl

flag

Carefully watch the long and short vowels as you read the blends, words and sentences.

flā	flē	flī	flō	flū
flă	flĕ	flĭ	flŏ	flŭ

fleet	flap	flick	flash	flute
float	flea	fled	flake	flip
flop	flee	flame	flag	fly

class	clam	club	clean	click
bluff	blast	bleak	bled	blame
bliss	blew	bless	blaze	black

Tim will wave and say bye.

It is time to go back home.

gl

glide

Carefully watch the long and short vowels as you read the blends, words and sentences.

glā	glē	glī	glō	glū
glă	glĕ	glĭ	glŏ	glŭ

glad	Glen	glum	glide	glove
glib	glaze	glee	glade	glut
glass	globe	gloat	gloss	glare

flake	flag	flute	flip	fly
clue	clap	close	clay	clip
bluff	blast	blow	bled	blame

Bill got the clue to win the game.

Did Glen see the new glove?

The long **E** - **e** vowel blends are: **e, ea, ee** and **ey**. Practice saying these with the different consonants and blends.

Chart 11 **41**

pl

pledge

Carefully watch the long and short vowels as you read the blends, words and sentences.

plā	plē	plī	plō	plū
plă	plĕ	plĭ	plŏ	plŭ

plot	plane	plug	place	play
plum	plate	pled	plain	plea
plan	plead	plus	plat	plop

blame	clue	plot	bled	class
flame	glue	blot	pled	glass
plane	blue	flop	fled	blast

The plate fell and broke.

Tim will try and fix the plate.

The long **I - i** vowel blends are: **i, ie, i_e** and **y**. Practice saying these with the different consonants and blends.

sl

sled

Carefully watch the long and short vowels as you read the blends, words and sentences.

slā	slē	slī	slō	slū
slă	slĕ	slĭ	slŏ	slŭ

slam	slave	sled	slew	slime
sleep	slate	slay	slide	slop
slap	slack	sleet	slim	sly

plain	plat	play	plea	plop
gloat	glum	glee	globe	glaze
fleet	flea	flap	float	flop

Deb will mix a cake.

The cake is the best.

Chart 11   43

br

broom

Carefully watch the long and short vowels as you read the blends, words and sentences.

brā	brē	brī	brō	brū
bră	brĕ	brĭ	brŏ	brŭ

brass	brain	broke	brag	brat
Brad	brake	breed	brave	brim
brush	bribe	bray	brick	broke

slay	slush	slew	slide	slim
plate	plain	plus	plug	plot
globe	glide	glee	glass	glut

Sal will use the broom to clean.

Fix the brake on my bike.

The long **O** - **o** vowel blends are: **o, oe, oa, o_e** and **ow**. Practice saying these with the different consonants and blends.

cr

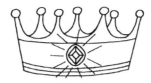

crown

Carefully watch the long and short vowels as you read the blends, words and sentences.

crā	crē	crī	crō	crū
cră	crĕ	crĭ	crŏ	crŭ

cry	crane	crate	creek	crisp
cream	crab	craze	crest	crude
cross	creap	creak	croak	crust

brave	brain	brick	broke	breed
slam	sly	slop	sled	slug
plum	plate	plod	plea	place

The creek is deep.

The frog will croak in the creek.

The long **U** - **u** vowel blends are: **u, ui, u_e** and **ew**. Practice saying these with the different consonants and blends.

Chart 11 **45**

dr

dress

Carefully watch the long and short vowels as you read the blends, words and sentences.

drā	drē	drī	drō	drū
dră	drĕ	drĭ	drŏ	drŭ

drum	drop	dry	drug	drip
dross	drill	drag	drain	drab
drove	dream	drive	drape	drone

glass	brake	crate	brew	fly
brass	flake	slate	flew	cry
class	Blake	plate	slew	sly

at	up	on	in	to
well	map	pup	big	top

Drop the drum in the hut.

Get the hat on the box.

fr

fry

Carefully watch the long and short vowels as you read the blends, words and sentences.

| frā | frē | frī | frō | frū |
| fră | frĕ | frĭ | frŏ | frŭ |

Froze	fret	free	fruit	freak
Fred	frail	frock	frog	Fran
fry	frost	frame	frill	friz

drag	drug	drip	drone	dream
crane	crab	creap	craft	craze
brim	broke	bribe	Brad	brew

Jim has a new glove.

He will make the play.

Jim can play

in the game.

Chart 11   47

gr

grasshopper

Carefully watch the long and short vowels as you read the blends, words and sentences.

grā	grē	grī	grō	grū
gră	grĕ	grĭ	grŏ	grŭ

grass	gray	green	grab	grub
grip	greet	grate	greed	grind
grain	grin	grace	grit	grub

sea	clock	drip	drug	drain
tea	block	flip	plug	slain
plea	flock	slip	slug	plain

beg	hem	mitt	Dick	red
hill	fed	kiss	jam	luck

Do you still remember these important words? They are: **a, the, and, to, I, into, come, what, do** and **two.**

pr

pray

Carefully watch the long and short vowels as you read the blends, words and sentences.

| prā | prē | prī | prō | prū |
| pră | prĕ | prĭ | prŏ | prŭ |

prime	prim	prod	press	pry
prop	prune	prick	prone	praise
pride	probe	prize	prose	pray

grab	greed	grit	grub	grin
fret	frame	frock	Fred	frill
dress	drab	drive	drug	drop

sad	toss	tab	had	cod
sock	Bill	hit	mess	mud

Fred will take the prize.

We pray to God.

Chart 11   49

tr

tractor

trā	trē	trī	trō	trū
tră	trĕ	trĭ	trŏ	trŭ

trade	tribe	trail	trace	tread
trick	truck	tree	trap	try
trust	trip	trim	tray	trash

pride	prim	prune	probe	prod
grip	greet	grub	grate	grope
frost	friz	frog	Fran	free

Pat will dig

and plant.

It is fun to see

the seeds grow.

sc

scale

Carefully watch the long and short vowels as you read the blends, words and sentences.

scā	scē	scī	scō	scū
scă	scĕ	scĭ	scŏ	scŭ

scat	scope	scab	scull	Scott
scale	Scot	scare	score	scorn
scan	scum	scone	scoff	scuff

truck	trip	trail	tree	trim
pride	pray	press	prune	prose
grass	grit	grade	grub	grow

The truck drove up the steep hill.

The truck will stop at the big tree.

Don't forget, when there are two vowels in a word, the first vowel says its long sound, and the second vowel is silent.

Chart 11   51

sk

skate

Carefully watch the long and short vowels as you read the blends, words and sentences.

skā	skē	skī	skō	skū
skă	skĕ	skĭ	skŏ	skŭ

skill	skit	skim	skin	skull
sky	skate	skip	skid	skew

scab	slug	skid	stop	beg
tab	plug	slid	flop	leg
flab	tug	grid	drop	Greg
drab	mug	lid	mop	Peg

Jan will play in the skit.

Her pal Jen will play in the skit.

Jan and Jen can make a play.

A lot of kids will be in the play.

sm

smell

Carefully watch the long and short vowels as you read the blends, words and sentences.

smā	smē	smī	smō	smū
smă	smĕ	smĭ	smŏ	smŭ

smile	smack	smug	smog	smote
smoke	smell	smite	smock	smew*

sky	skit	skate	skull	skew
scale	scum	scoff	scat	scuff
trade	tray	tread	trim	truck
prize	prim	pry	praise	prop

Tom will sleep with Buff.

It is fun to sleep with Buff.

Buff has a clean hut.

*Smew is a small Eurasian duck that dives for fish.

Chart 11 **53**

sn

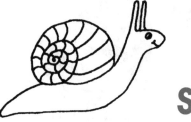

snail

Carefully watch the long and short vowels as you read the blends, words and sentences.

snā	snē	snī	snō	snū
snă	snĕ	snĭ	snŏ	snŭ

snake	snore	snap	sniff	snug
snag	sneak	snip	snare	snuff
snipe	snub	snow	snob	snail

smoke	smack	smell	smug	smite
sky	skit	skate	skim	skip
scam	Scott	scull	scare	score

Do not play by the hole.

It is not safe to play by the hole.

Important sight words which help to connect sentences are: **says, put, does, are** and **you**.

54   Chart 11

sp

spider

Carefully watch the long and short vowels as you read the blends, words and sentences.

spā	spē	spī	spō	spū
spă	spĕ	spĭ	spŏ	spŭ

space	spare	spell	spill	spoke
spade	speak	spice	spin	spot
span	speed	spike	spit	spume

time	play	truck	tree	drop
slime	pray	stuck	free	flop
grime	fray	pluck	flee	crop

Pam will give Tab a ride.

Pam will speak to Tab.

"Sit up Tab,"

is what Pam will say.

Chart 11 **55**

st

20¢

stamp

Carefully watch the long and short vowels as you read the blends, words and sentences.

stā	stē	stī	stō	stū
stă	stĕ	stĭ	stŏ	stŭ

stone	stove	stop	stare	step
state	stun	still	stay	stuff
stain	stick	stem	steal	stun

spot	spill	speak	space	speed
you	says	put	does	are
snake	snob	snip	snug	snow

Will you lick a stamp?

I need a stamp for the mail.

I will send a note to dad.

He will get the note at his job.

SW

swim

Carefully watch the long and short vowels as you read the blends, words and sentences.

swā	swē	swī	swō	swū
swă	swĕ	swĭ	swŏ	swŭ

swipe	sweep	sweet	swag	Swiss
swim	swam	sway	swine	swell

still	stay	stun	stove	step
spade	spice	spume	spin	spell
the	and	I	come	what
snap	sneak	sniff	snail	snuff

Tim and I can swim a mile.

I can swim a mile and not stop.

Many words become plurals by adding **s** to the end. A plural means more than one. For example: bike -- bikes

Chart 11 **57**

Consonant Blend Review

Listen for the consonant blends as you say each of these words.

bl	cl	fl	gl	pl
bluff	close	fled	glad	plot
bless	claim	flake	glee	plus
blip	clash	flip	glade	place

cub – cube	calm – clame
Tim – time	bled – bleed
black – Blake	pat – pay
glob – globe	pled – plead
glad – glade	lad – laid

Dad will taste the meal.

He likes it a lot.

Deb will wait for a taste.

Mom will feed Deb next.

Consonant Blend Review

Listen for the consonant blends as you say each of these words.

sl	br	cr	dr	fr
slime	broke	crane	drag	frog
slate	brim	crest	drill	frill
sleet	brat	crust	drove	frost

plum – plume	Brad – braid
slop – slope	bit – bite
Fred – freed	pin – pine
ran – rain	bread – breed
slat – slate	slim – slime

Can Tom skate on the hill?

He can go fast.

Mom will tell Tom to go slow.

He may fall and hit his head.

Chart 11   59

Consonant Blend Review

Listen for the consonant blends as you say each of these words.

gr	pr	tr	sc	sk
grass	prize	tribe	scale	sky
grate	pray	trap	scare	skid
greet	prop	trash	scoff	skull

grim – grime	fed – feed
prim – prime	grad – grade
red – read	pin – pine
mad – made	plat – plate
quit – quite	rip – ripe

Ben will pray by the bed.

Tom will pray at the meal.

We can speak to God,

if we take the time to pray.

Consonant Blend Review

Listen for the consonant blends as you say each of these words.

sm	sn	sp	st	sw
smile	snap	span	stove	swipe
smell	sneak	spice	step	swell
smog	sniff	spot	stem	swiss

snip – snipe	spin – spine
bat – bait	can – cane
sped – speed	spit – spite
pan – pane	cop – cope
kit – kite	cut – cute

It is time to eat a meal.

Do not make a mess.

Chart 11   **61**

dw   squ   tw

dwell   squat   twine

Here are a few more consonant blends to learn.
Be careful as you sound these out.

squire	squeeze	twist
twins	dwell	tweed
squeak	squat	twice
squib	twig	dwine

drive	trap	gloat	prone	what
breed	put	dross	plum	slack
class	smoke	does	dream	Mom
grate	Fred	skid	flee	clock

The twig is big.

It is as big as a stick.

Can you tie the twine on the twig?

The twins will twist the twine on the twig.

62   Chart 12

scr spl spr str

scrub splat spray strap

Here are a few more consonant blends to learn.
Be careful as you sound these out.

scrap	scribe	spray
split	scrape	splat
stroke	scream	stream
sprain	spree	street

glade	free	come	it	blame
brim	says	toast	flip	slop
do	grace	ply	drain	at
score	drape	prune	slate	Coke

Pat will go on a run.

He will take care

not to sprain his leg.

Chart 12 **63**

ll   ff

doll

cuff

The next several pages teach consonant blends which generally appear at the end of a word. Practice reading these words.

quill	gull	still	well
bell	fell	dull	smell

stiff	huff	stuff	puff
staff	cliff	muff	Biff

fan	fret	cluck	hill	clog
clan	pet	buck	Bill	hog
pan	set	puck	pill	frog
bran	wet	truck	mill	smog

Rule: When a word has a short vowel sound, usually the consonants **s**, **l**, **f** and **z** will be doubled.

SS  ZZ

bass   buzz

This page teaches consonant blends which generally appear at the end of a word. Practice reading these words and sentences.

press	fizz	fuss	miss
fuzz	glass	buzz	muss
dress	pass	less	jazz

bell	slam	kid	God	cliff
tree	jug	cone	stuff	drain
jam	gull	place	lab	dot
brick	red	smell	frost	tie

Make a list of what to get.

We need to go to the shop.

Three other double consonant blends are **bb**, **gg** and **tt**. These blends are used in words such as **ebb**, **egg** and mi**tt**.

Chart 13 **65**

ck

sock

This page teaches consonant blends which generally appear at the end of a word. Practice reading these words and sentences.

quack	track	lick	block
buck	brick	lock	truck
jack	wick	sock	dock

fuzz	press	gull	staff
bless	jazz	cuff	fell

Tom will put his socks on his feet.

His socks are big and red.

Tom likes his red socks.

He will lock his socks in the truck.

The **ck** blend belongs with the double consonants. Whenever a short vowel word ends with a **k** sound, it is the **ck** that must be there.

sk **sp**

desk   **gra**sp

This page teaches consonant blends which generally appear at the end of a word. Practice reading these words and sentences.

de**sk**	hu**sk**	ga**sp**	cri**sp**
gra**sp**	wi**sp**	cla**sp**	ri**sk**

Mu**tt**	s**e**ll	fix	mi**tt**	w**i**ck
hi**ll**	ki**ck**	lo**ck**	f**e**d	h**a**d
lid	ki**ss**	sip	hu**ll**	hi**ss**
bu**ck**	vim	ti**ff**	blo**ck**	l**a**p
wig	**e**gg	men	n**a**p	tr**a**ck

Bill will sweep up the fuzz by the bed.

He has a new mop.

It is his job to clean the mess.

His mom is glad he did the job.

Chart 13   **67**

st   lf

cast   **golf**

This page teaches consonant blends which generally appear at the end of a word. Practice reading these words and sentences.

vest	golf	vast	mast
gulf	self	pest	elf

bet	quit	lock	cub	dam
get	sit	dock	hub	ham
let	pit	mock	rub	jam
met	mitt	rock	sub	ram
net	fit	sock	tub	yam

Pam had ham and an egg.

Jen fed Al an egg.

Rex can sell ham.

Do you need an egg?

lk   lp

elk   help

This page teaches consonant blends which generally appear at the end of a word. Practice reading these words and sentences.

milk	help	bulk	silk
elk	yelp	gulp	pulp

ask	risk	quack	puff	buzz
bell	jazz	stuff	wick	splat
mast	asp	dock	golf	lisp
scribe	pass	fuss	self	scrap
jack	spree	dusk	dull	block

Pete lost the game.

He tried real hard,

but did not win.

He will bat the next day.

Chart 13   **69**

lt **mp**

quilt **jump**

This page teaches consonant blends which generally appear at the end of a word. Practice reading these words and sentences.

tilt	dump	hilt	damp
camp	cult	lamp	halt

gull	yam	bulk	pot	silk
wisp	yelp	mast	elf	the
van	quill	husk	vest	buck
help	pop	was	gulp	come

Dick has a big lump of clay.

He will build a nice pot.

Here are some other consonant ending blends. **lb** - bu**lb**, **ld** - he**ld**, **lm** - fi**lm**, **dge** - fu**dge**, **nce** - fe**nce**, and **nse** - te**nse**.

nd   **ct**

2+2=4

band   **fact**

This page teaches consonant blends which generally appear at the end of a word. Practice reading these words and sentences.

act	end	tact	pact
fend	duct	mend	hand

tilt	cult	hilt	halt
clamp	limp	dump	slump
milk	elk	bulk	silk
yelp	pulp	gulp	help
elf	golf	self	gulf

My hand has a bump.

I hit it on my truck.

I cried, but my Mom kissed it.

My Mom is kind.

Chart 13   **71**

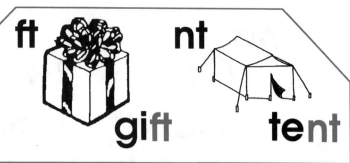

ft · gift   nt · tent

This page teaches consonant blends which generally appear at the end of a word. Practice reading these words and sentences.

left	tint	rent	lift
punt	raft	aft	hunt

creep	brain	cut	ox	bin
sleep	slain	gut	box	fin
steep	plain	nut	fox	pin
sweep	Cain	rut	pox	sin
jeep	Spain	but	sox	tin

Sam gave a gift to Jan.

It was a card and a dress.

Jan was glad to get the dress.

Jan will put the dress on the bed.

pt **xt**

wept **te**xt

This page teaches consonant blends which generally appear at the end of a word. Practice reading these words and sentences.

slept	kept	text
next	apt	crept

act	mast	tot	raft	buzz
bass	bust	rent	mend	last
tint	duct	elk	husk	aft
camp	ten	held	film	staff
pulp	bulb	fast	egg	hand

Don will jump and get wet.

He will spring off his feet.

Don will fly into the waves.

Chart 13 **73**

ng   nk

ring   drink

This page teaches consonant blends which generally appear at the end of a word. Practice reading these words and sentences.

bang	wink	king	hunk
bank	lung	ink	bang

apt	cult	act	tint	hunt
pact	left	band	raft	clump
aft	fend	text	kept	fact
tilt	crept	clamp	hand	next

May I have a drink of juice?

I like grape juice the best.

Do you still remember these consonant blends? **lb** - bu**lb**, **ld** - he**ld**, **lm** - fi**lm**, **dge** - fu**dge**, **nce** - fe**nce**, and **nse** - te**nse**.

sh

ship

Listen for the different consonant blends and digraphs as you say each of these words.

brush	bush	mash	wish
fish	mush	shut	dish
splash	shop	rush	shed

punt	bang	game	wink	dress
next	fake	bank	kept	lung

The tot will splash in the tub.

He will wash with soap.

Take care not to get wet,

if you wash the tot.

A consonant digraph has two consonants that make one sound. Examples of digraphs are **sh**, **ch**, **th** and **wh**.

Chart 12 **75**

ch

church

Listen for the different consonant blends and digraphs as you say each of these words.

check	chop	chug	chex
chess	much	such	chat
rich	chill	chum	chip

bank	load	snake	shut	lung
brush	mush	ink	time	shed
smoke	hunk	fish	bang	mash
splash	shop	well	wish	bake

The chick is a duck.

The duck says quack.

The chick is wet.

He is a wet duck.

76   Chart 12

wh

whale

Listen for the different consonant blends and digraphs as you say each of these words.

whale	when	whip	wheel
what	which	whim	wheeze
why	whim	wheat	white

chess	shut	chum	chill	wish
brush	much	dish	shed	rich

What did the white whale do?

Did he swim to sea?

Let us get a boat and find him.

The sea is the place the whale will be.

Remember, a digraph has two consonants that make one sound. For example: **sh - ship**, **ch - chick**, **wh - why**, and **th - then**.

Chart 12 **77**

th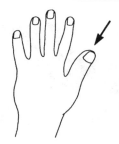

thumb

Listen for the different consonant blends and digraphs as you say each of these words.

them	that	this	brother
then	the	father	than

with	thank	bath	path
thing	think	thin	Beth

Pete will help his mother.

He has a big rake.

Mother will take the load,

and dump it in the trash.

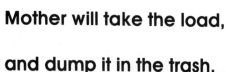

The digraph **th** makes two different sounds. The first sound makes a noise, **th** as in **them**; the second sound makes a whisper, **th** as in **think**.

Consonant Blend Review

Listen for the consonant blends as you say each of these words.

ll	ff	ss	zz	ck
quill	puff	bass	jazz	block
bell	cliff	dress	fizz	dock
doll	staff	muss	fuzz	duck

bug	den	jet	wick
pig	fell	Ken	yes
fun	cat	hug	fix
man	nap	rip	quiz
lap	gun	tan	Ted

The day is great.

I will play in the sun.

I will ride my bike and

talk to Beth.

God has made this great day.

Chart 13   79

Consonant Blend Review

Listen for the consonant blends as you say each of these words.

sk	sp	st	lf	lk
desk	clasp	vest	elf	milk
husk	crisp	pest	golf	elk
risk	gasp	mast	self	bulk

bud	drum	rack	Bob
lick	pot	sad	hen
Josh	nod	wax	gag
hall	mat	yam	Deb
fist	log	fox	pen

My cat is not well.

She must be sick.

My mom will get the vet.

He will make Puff well.

Consonant Blend Review

Listen for the consonant blends as you say each of these words.

lp	lt	mp	nd	ct
pulp	quilt	jump	fend	pact
help	tilt	lamp	mend	fact
gulp	halt	damp	band	duct

yum	quill	bib	list
win	tot	fat	nick
vat	sod	kill	pit
sing	dip	jug	God
run	cot	hem	jazz

Jim will fix the meal.

He likes to bake

on the stove.

What is for lunch, Jim?

It smells great!

Chart 13   81

Consonant Blend Review

Listen for the consonant blends as you say each of these words.

ft	nt	pt	xt	ng	nk
left	tent	slept	next	ring	drink
gift	bent	kept	text	sing	hunk
raft	hunt	apt	next	lung	wink

bluff	trace	drop	Scott
cluck	plain	slide	flap
brass	croak	click	skip
Glen	frock	glare	brave
prim	grace	scan	creak

Jan will sweep the step.

Then she will clean the rug.

Jan likes this job.

Jan is a big help.

Digraph Blend Review

Listen for the consonant blends as you say each of these words.

sh	ch	wh	th	th
shed	chess	which	them	with
dish	much	when	father	thing
shop	chex	whale	this	bath

skate	spin	twice	squeeze
street	swipe	stay	twins
stun	smell	snip	sway
scrape	stream	spume	spice
snail	split	spree	scream

What time is it?

Do you have a clock?

I am late for a date with Nate.

Nate will not wait.

He will go if I am late.

Chart 12 **83**

ld   nd   gh

child   kind   light

Here are a few consonant blends where the **i** is long when followed by **ld**, **nd** or **gh**.

light	fight	find
grind	kind	night
right	wild	bind
mild	sight	flight

risk	king	pit	jig	bid
inch	ship	dill	rip	drill
ring	his	Rick	hiss	six

The blind child was mild.

She did not like to fight.

She will find it is right to be kind.

When the letters **gh** follow the long **i**, the **gh** sound is silent.

ld   st   th   ll   lt

co**ld** po**st** bo**th** ro**ll** co**lt**

Here are a few consonant blends where the **o** is long when followed by **ld, st, th, ll** or **lt**.

bo**lt**	ho**ld**	mo**ld**
stro**ll**	mo**st**	bo**ld**
fo**ld**	po**ll**	to**ll**
bo**th**	co**lt**	ho**st**

B**o**b	ch**o**p	l**o**g	**o**n	p**o**t
l**o**ck	b**o**ng	T**o**m	h**o**p	b**o**x
off	s**o**d	bl**o**ck	bl**o**nd	fr**o**th

The colt is not in the fold.

Did you close the gate and lock the bolt?

The short vowel rule teaches that the vowel is usually short when it comes at the beginning or between two consonants. These pages show some of the exceptions.

Chart 14   85

ou

hound

This page teaches a blend which makes a sound you may say when you are hurt. Practice reading these words and sentences.

count	hound	house	pout
mouth	scout	mouse	pound
blouse	round	hour	snout

load	**coal**	**crow**	**host**
bold	**snow**	**soap**	**float**
loaf	**most**	**mold**	**grow**
oak	**boat**	**coast**	**blown**

The old hound lay by the side of the road.

His snout could smell a mouse.

A growl came from his throat,

and with a bound he was in the house.

OW

COW

This page teaches a blend which makes a sound you may say when you are hurt. Practice reading these words and sentences.

vowels	clown	brown	town
owl	tower	power	crown
flower	cow	growl	down

robe	joke	hoe	cone
doe	broke	whole	tone
rode	foe	home	zone
poem	pole	Rome	toe

The brown hound had a crown

and lived up in a tower.

He went down town to see the clown

and pick for him a flower.

Chart 14 **87**

ä

jar

The consonant **r** has a strong sound. When it comes after a vowel, it changes the vowel sound. Practice these words and sentences.

ark	cart	arch	car
far	Mark	part	park
barn	dart	march	art

trap	trash	sand	slash
draft	grass	tram	bland
spam	stab	drag	brat
plant	camp	act	batch

Park the cart in the barn

and march far into the arch.

Drive the car to the park,

and dart in for a part.

corn

The **o** sound is another vowel which is changed by the **r**. Practice reading these words and sentences.

core	thorn	fork	horn
stork	storm	horse	pork
born	corn	cord	porch

round	flower	clouds	hour
mouth	count	snout	down
owl	cow	mouse	vowels
down	clown	pound	tower

Mark will race his skate board.

He can go real fast.

Mark best take care,

   or he will trip and crash.

Chart 14 **89**

oo

shoot

The **oo** says the long **u** vowel sound in these words. Listen for the blends as you say each of the words.

goose	doom	booth	spoon
hoot	roof	food	scoop
boot	tool	zoom	broom

shun	shut	blunt	slush
but	puff	brush	trunk
mud	lung	glut	plum
bug	gulf	plug	hung

Jill has made a booth.

She wants to sell drinks.

Many would come if she

had more food.

Then her sales would zoom.

oo u o ou

book put wolf would

Listen for the blends as you say each of these words and sentences.

cook	shook	push	could
wolves	wood	full	bush
hook	put	bush	hood
should	pull	wolf	would

cube	tune	juice	blew
suit	drew	stew	mule
pew	tube	fuse	fruit

The wind blew and shook the wood.

The wolf will howl at the moon.

Many blends make up the important long vowel **u** sound. They are: **ew** - screw, **u_e** - tube, **ui** - fruit, **ue** - glue, and **oo** - zoo. What are some other long **u** words?

Chart 14   91

oi   oy

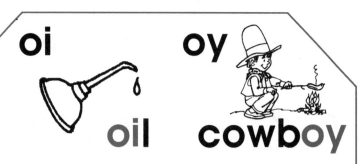

oil   cowboy

Listen for the different consonant blends and digraphs as you say each of these words.

boy	soil	coins	voice
foil	Joy	toy	Roy
point	noise	coil	joint

push	should	pull	hook	could
hood	bush	book	wood	wolf

The small boy is Roy.

He got a new toy.

Joy gave Roy the toy.

It made a loud noise.

Rule: A diphthong is a sound made up of two vowels blended together to make one sound. The blends **oi** and **oy** are diphthongs.

er   ir   ur

verse   bird   turtle

Listen for the blends as you say each of these words.

bird	nurse	curl	turn
purse	skirt	burn	hurt
verse	girl	first	dirt
church	fern	third	stir

owl	count	crown	pout
blouse	power	hour	town
growl	snout	flower	mouse

The turtle ran in a race.

He made a turn for the worse.

He did not finish first, but third.

When **e**, **i** and **u** are followed by an **r**, they make the same sound. They sound just like a rooster when it crows.

Chart 15   93

(w)or ear

world earth

Two more ways to spell the **er** sound are **ear** and **(w)or**. Listen for the blends in the words.

learn	words	early	work
heard	worth	world	worm

turn	nurse	cook	girl
could	toy	dirt	verse
boy	bush	pull	noise
hood	joint	foil	wolves
put	bird	first	full

God made the whole world.

The earth shows that He is good.

Rule: A long word may be divided between two consonants. The two consonants will usually keep the first vowel short. For example: bet-ter, gig-gle, pad-dle, lit-tle.

ô

frog

Another sound which the **o** makes is **ô** as in dog. Listen for the blends as you say each of these words.

log	cross	hog	long
cloth	dog	cost	frost
moth	off	soft	frog

w**or**se	w**or**th	l**ear**n	sp**ee**d
Bl**a**k**e**	sl**a**t	wh**ea**t	bluff
h**o**p**e**	h**ear**d	pl**a**t**e**	pl**e**d
r**ea**d	c**u**t	sl**o**p**e**	scr**ea**m

The frog will hop on a log.

He must hop if he is to cross.

The frog will stop to eat a moth.

He will hop off to hide from a dog.

Chart 15   **95**

al aw au

ball draw haul

Listen for the blends as you say each of these words.

claw	hawk	fault	hall
ball	small	chalk	flaw
draw	salt	malt	halt
jaw	paw	tall	haul

doom	roof	broom	book	look
hood	zoom	spoon	tool	scoop

Paul can hit the ball.

It does not matter

if we are small or tall.

If we try hard, we all can hit a ball.

Remember the sound of ô as in frog. The vowel **a** makes the same sound when it is followed by an **l, w** or **u**.

augh ough

caught fought

Listen for the blends as you say each of these words.

caught	naughty	fought	bought
daughter	taught	sought	fraught

ball	off	long	small
log	hog	tall	cross
soft	cloth	frost	fault
cost	malt	moth	jaw
salt	frog	haul	dog

The daughter was naughty.

She was not kind to her mother.

Children are to obey their parents.

The blends ô - frog, al - ball, au - haul, aw - saw, augh - caught and ough - fought all make the same sound.

Chart 15 **97**

are arr air

bare carrot chair

This lesson teaches the **âr** sound as in squ**are**.
Listen for the blends as you say these words.

carry	stairs	carrot	Larry
hair	care	chair	mare
square	fair	dare	rare

log	malt	taught	sought	dog
cost	fault	draw	frog	tall
claw	ball	frost	fought	fraught

A hare named Larry sat on the chair.

He had to carry his carrots up the stairs.

He did not think it was fair,

that he had to give his carrots to the mare.

Besides **âr** as in squ**are**, do you remember the other **ar** sound you have learned? It is **är** as in **ar**m.

err ear ere

berry pear where

This lesson teaches the **âr** sound as in squ**are**.
Listen for the blends as you say these words.

bear	there	berry
cherry	pear	merry
tear	where	swear

bru**sh**	fa**th**er	di**sh**	wi**th**
chum	**wh**im	**ch**ess	**wh**eat
whale	**ch**at	**wh**ite	su**ch**
thank	**sh**ip	**th**em	ru**sh**

Where did the ball go?

Harry did not see it in the air.

"There it is," the boys cried.

But Harry did not get there.

Chart 15 **99**

c

city

This lesson teaches that the consonant **c** usually makes the soft sound of **s** when **e**, **i** or **y** come after the letter.

race	rice	lace	mice
fence	city	ice	slice
circle	pencil	face	pace

club	click	cream	crust
cup	cat	can	claim

The mice had a race to the city.

They went at a fast pace.

They ran on a fence, and slid on the ice,

but stopped when they came to the place.

The consonant **c** makes the hard sound of **k** when the vowels **a**, **o** and **u** come after it. For example: **c**at, **c**ot and **c**ut.

g

giraffe

This lesson teaches that the consonant **g** usually makes the soft sound of **j** when **e**, **i** or **y** come after the letter.

badge	engine	hinge
gel	gem	large
bridge	giraffe	pledge

God	glee	gas	gill
get	glare	gum	grass

Penny will pledge to the flag.

We are one nation under God.

It is an honor to live

in the United States.

The consonant **g** makes the hard sound of **g** when the vowels **a**, **o** and **u** come after it. For example: **gag**, **got** and **gull**.

Chart 15   **101**

kn   wr

knife   **wr**ite

Two other important digraphs to learn are **kn** as in **kn**ot and **wr** as in **wr**ite. The **k** and **w** are both silent when followed by **n** and **r**.

knee	wring	knot	wrinkle
wren	knock	knuckle	knife
kneel	write	wrong	wrench

ra**c**e	bri**dg**e	mi**c**e	lar**g**e
gel	i**c**e	hin**g**e	fen**c**e
sli**c**e	**c**ity	**c**ircle	pa**c**e
giraffe	en**g**ine	**g**em	pled**g**e

The wren said, "There is a wrinkle

in my feather."

The mother said, "I will write you a letter."

Get a knife and knock the knot

off your knuckle.

ing

cooking

A word can be changed by adding a <u>suffix</u> to its ending. The first suffix to learn is **ing**.

picking	looking	going	adding
telling	talking	rolling	flying
puffing	seeing	praying	ringing

knock	**wr**ing	**kn**ee	**wr**ong
b**ear**	p**ear**	merry	th**ere**
h**air**	m**are**	carry	f**air**
c**augh**t	s**ough**t	t**augh**t	b**ough**t

The boy was not looking

as to where he was going.

He came to a hill

and down he went rolling.

Chart 15 **103**

y

sky day rocky

This lesson teaches the different ways the letter **y** can be pronounced.

cry	day	May	penny
happy	fly	baby	say
dry	rocky	hilly	try

read**ing**	jump**ing**	pick**ing**	bow**ling**
wren	**kn**eel	**kn**ock	**wr**ing
fa**c**e	sli**c**e	hin**g**e	lar**g**e
l**ear**n	h**ear**d	w**or**d	w**or**m
b**ir**d	n**ur**se	sk**ir**t	th**ir**d

When the **y** is the only vowel in a word, it has a long **i** sound as in fly. When the **y** follows another vowel, it is usually silent as in day. When there are other vowels in the word, the **y** has the long sound of **e** as in baby.

er

work**er**

A word can be changed by adding a <u>suffix</u> to its ending. This lesson teaches the **er** suffix.

talker	fusser	thinker	climber
jumper	eater	singer	walker
helper	sleeper	player	shopper

happ**y**	bab**y**	penn**y**	rock**y**
dr**y**	hill**y**	tr**y**	Ma**y**
oil	s**oi**l	R**oy**	j**oi**nt
p**u**t	p**u**ll	w**oo**d	w**ou**ld

If you jump you are a jumper.

If you sing you are a singer.

If you play you are a player.

If you think you are a thinker.

Chart 15 105

ies

copies

This lesson teaches how a word can be made plural, (meaning more than one), when the last letter is a **y**.

toy**s**	cit**ies**	boy**s**	part**ies**
pon**ies**	pray**s**	stor**ies**	pay**s**
play**s**	pupp**ies**	turkey**s**	fl**ies**

talk**er**	climb**er**	sleep**er**	help**er**
walk**er**	sing**er**	eat**er**	writ**er**

Look at those puppies.

They are fun to watch.

The puppies like to play with toys.

Rule: Just add an **s** to the word if the **y** comes after a vowel -- toy**s**. Change the **y** to an **i** and add **es** if the **y** comes after a consonant -- part**ies**.

Mother

Sometimes the **o** makes the short sound of **u**, as this lesson teaches.

other	some	son	shove
brother	of	ton	come
from	front	dove	glove

suds	bus	tug	under
number	yum	bunny	hutch
up	scuff	umpire	butter
drug	lump	drum	slug

The umpire called a strike,

and the batter was out.

Get your glove and your brother.

It is time to go home to Mother.

Chart 15   **107**

a

alert

In these words, the beginning **a** has the short sound of **u**. Practice reading these words and sentences.

awake	along	ahead	asleep
alike	apart	ago	arose
alive	away	avoid	astray

of	fr**o**nt	s**o**n	t**o**n	d**o**ve
cr**y**	bab**y**	sa**y**	fr**y**	da**y**
knee	**kn**ock	**kn**ife	**kn**ot	**kn**eel
write	**wr**inkle	**wr**en	**wr**ong	**wr**ing

A long time ago,

a lady fell asleep.

She awoke when a prince kissed her,

and swept her off her feet.

mb bt gu bu

limb doubt guess build

Here are a few more silent letter blends to learn. Carefully read these words.

dumb	lamb	guess	climb
build	guilt	comb	debt
guest	doubt	guide	tomb

alone	**a**loud	**a**part	**a**long
asleep	**a**head	**a**fraid	**a**like
lad**ies**	way**s**	day**s**	part**ies**
fl**ies**	key**s**	sk**ies**	play**s**

Jesus arose from the dead,

and left the tomb empty.

In some words the letters, **gh**, **h** and **t** are silent. For example: **gh** as in fi**gh**t, **h** as in **h**our, and **t** as in of**t**en.

Chart 15   **109**

ph   gh

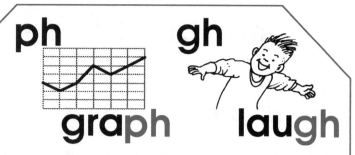

graph   laugh

This lesson teaches that **gh** and **ph** sometimes have the sound of **f**.

tough	phone	phase	laugh
Ralph	rough	cough	phrase
phony	photo	graphic	Phil

fight	coat	fame	blue	jerk
sight	note	blame	glue	term
might	float	shame	true	herd
right	wrote	tame	clue	term

Phil laughed on the phone to his friend.

He was talking to Ralph on the other end.

Come on, let us go and see the show,

and do not forget to bring Glen.

Reading Review

Carefully say the words and then read the story. Look for the new words in the story.

death	be-lieve	heav-en	wis-dom
brought	per-ish	thank-ful	Sav-ior

The Bible

Are you able to tell me which is the best book in the world? Yes, that is easy. The Bible is the best book in the world, and it is the book we should like best.

It is the only book in the world which is able to save our souls, now and forever.

It is the Word of God to men, telling us that man was first made good and holy, but that he was led to sin. Now all men are sinners.

It also tells us that God loved the world so much that He sent His son Jesus, who came and gave His life to save sinners.

All who believe in the Son of God as their Savior shall not perish, but be saved from sin, and be brought to glory in heaven. For this, we should be thankful.

Let us learn to read well that we may soon be able to read the Bible. We will learn true wisdom from it.

Reading Review

Carefully say the words and then read the story. Look for the new words in the story.

chief	peo-ple	col-ors
wealth	cat-tle	coun-try
an-gry	seized	jeal-ous

The Story of Joseph -- Part 1

In a country far away from here, there lived an old man who had twelve sons. He loved them all very much, but he loved two of them more than all the rest.

The names of these two were Joseph and Benjamin. He loved Joseph most, and for him he made a coat of many colors. The other brothers were angry at this, and were jealous of Joseph.

In that country, their flocks and herds were the chief wealth of the people. Jacob, the father, had a great many cattle and sheep. The brothers were shepherds, and had to take care of them.

They were once far away with their flocks. Their father had not heard from them for some time, so he sent Joseph to

112

see how they were doing.

As soon as his brothers saw him coming, they said among themselves, "Come, let us kill him." But the eldest brother said, "No; let us put him into a deep pit."

When Joseph came to them, they seized the poor lad, stripped off his coat of many colors, and threw him into the pit.

beast	suf-fer	de-ceive
doubt	tri-als	mer-chants
wrath	a-fraid	mean-time
troub-le	pris-on	wick-ed

The Story of Joseph -- Part 2

Shortly after this, they saw some merchants, who were going to a country called Egypt. They thought it would be a good plan to sell Joseph to these people, who would take him far away. Then he would never trouble them again.

Thus these wicked brothers sold poor Joseph; but after they had done so, they were afraid of their father's wrath. They made up their minds to deceive their father.

They took Joseph's coat and dipped it in some blood, and then brought it to their father. They said that they had found it this way, and that some wild beast must have killed him.

Jacob did not doubt what they told him, and wept many days for his son.

But Joseph, in the meantime, had been taken off to Egypt and was sold for a slave.

He had to suffer a great many trials and was once put in prison, but in all his troubles he never forgot God. He continued to pray and put his trust in Him.

At last, he was brought before the king. Joseph became so useful to him that he was made ruler over the king's house, and then over all the land.

All this time, he had never spoken to his poor father. Although Joseph was a great ruler in Egypt, he did not forget his family, nor did he wish to do his brothers any harm.

Reading Review

Carefully say the words and then read the story. Look for the new words in the story.

face	wag-ons	be-cause
peace	a-live	fam-ine
a-rose	mon-ey	prom-ise

The Story of Joseph -- Part 3

Now a great famine arose in all those countries. No one had any corn to eat. Joseph, who had been told by God what was to come, had laid up great stores of food. Everyone came to him to buy corn.

During this time, Joseph's brothers also came. They did not know Joseph, although he knew them at once.

When they had bought the corn, they returned home again. They became afraid, for they found that their money had been put back into their sacks.

Joseph had spoken to them as if he were angry. He asked about their father and younger brother. He made them promise to bring Benjamin with them when they returned.

Reading Review

To make sure that they would do so, Joseph kept one of them back. This made their father very sad once again.

They soon had to go back to Egypt for more corn. They took with them Benjamin and more money. They told Joseph how they had found their money in their sacks.

Joseph acted as if he did not know them, wishing to test them. After a while he told them he was their brother. At this they were much afraid. Joseph was not angry, and sent them away happy.

Joseph also sent wagons with goods for Jacob and all his people. The king gave him a large tract of land for his family. There they lived with their flocks and herds in peace and plenty.

When Jacob heard that Joseph was still alive, he could not believe it. When the wagons came, he and his family were taken to Egypt. Jacob knew that God had protected his son.

When Jacob finally saw Joseph again, he cried out, "Now let me die, since I have seen thy face, because thou art yet alive."

Reading Review

Carefully say the words and then read the story. Look for the new words in the story.

walk-ing	fur-ther	safe-ty
mud-dy	hard-ly	trav-eled

The Blind Man and the Lame Man

A blind man was walking along a muddy road, and at last could get no further.

He met with a lame man, and begged him to guide him over the bad road.

"How can I do that," replied the lame man, "since I am hardly able to drag myself along?"

"But as you seem to be very strong, if you will carry me, we will travel through life together."

"I will then warn you of anything that may be in your way: your feet shall be my feet, and my eyes yours."

"With all my heart," said the blind man: "let us help each other in that way."

So taking his lame mate on his back, they traveled on with safety and pleasure.

Reading Review

neigh-bor   a-ny-bod-y   hap-pened

ev-ery-bod-y   dar-ling   temp-ta-tion

Thou God Seest Me

A kind neighbor sent Lucy's mother some beautiful pears. They were piled up in a low glass dish, with their pretty, plump cheeks smiling at everybody that passed.

When Lucy saw the pears, she ran up to the table to look at them. The next thing she did was to take one in her hand. Then she looked all around the room to see if anybody was there.

"Nobody will see me," thought Lucy. She was about to put the pear into her pocket when she returned it to the dish. She then skipped out of the room, without another look at the pears.

That night before she went to bed, she told her dad all that had happened. "What made you put the pear back, darling?" asked her father.

"Because that little verse, 'Thou God

Reading Review

seest me,' which I learned today in school, rang so loud in my ears that ! had to return it."

"Dear Lucy," said her father, kissing her. "I hope that little verse will help you to run away from every temptation, just as it did from this one."

hal-lowed	debt-ors	pow-er
heav-en	de-liv-er	temp-ta-tion

The Lord's Prayer

Our Father who art in heaven, hallowed be Thy name. Thy kingdom come. Thy will be done on earth, as it is in heaven. Give us this day our daily bread. And forgive us our debts, as we forgive our debtors. And lead us not into temptation, but deliver us from evil. For Thine is the kingdom, and the power, and the glory, forever. Amen

Reading Chart 1

a	**a**nt	n	**n**est
b	**b**ug	o	**o**strich
c	**c**at	p	**p**in
d	**d**uck	qu	**qu**ilt
e	**e**gg	r	**r**ing
f	**f**an	s	**s**eal
g	**g**um	t	**t**urtle
h	**h**at	u	**u**mpire
i	**i**ndian	v	**v**an
j	**j**et	w	**w**alrus
k	**k**ite	x	bo**x**
l	**l**amp	y	**y**arn
m	**m**op	z	**z**ebra

Reading Chart 2

Short Vowels		Long Vowels	
ă	ant astronaut	ā	acorn able
ĕ	egg engine	ē	eagle eat
ĭ	indian igloo	ī	ice idol
ŏ	ostrich otter	ō	overalls open
ŭ	umpire umbrella	ū	uniform unit

Reading Chart 3

Practice saying these consonant blends.

s   **t**   **b**

	s	t	b
a	s a	t a	b a
e	s e	t e	b e
i	s i	t i	b i
o	s o	t o	b o
u	s u	t u	b u

sat	tab	bat
set	toss	bet
sit	tub	bit
sob	tot	but

Rule: When a word has only one vowel and it comes at the beginning or between two consonants, the vowel is usually short.

Reading Chart 4

Practice saying these consonant blends.			
	h	**f**	**m**
a	h a	f a	m a
e	h e	f e	m e
i	h i	f i	m i
o	h o	f o	m o
u	h u	f u	m u

hit	fuss	mat
hot	fat	met
ham	fib	mob
hem	fit	moss

Tom	tuff	bum	mist
sub	has	bat	toss
mast	Bob	tub	Sam
bit	fast	sob	sum
bass	set	but	sat

123

Reading Chart 5

Practice saying these consonant blends.

c-k   d   j

a	c a	d a	j a
e	k e	d e	j e
i	k i	d i	j i
o	c o	d o	j o
u	c u	d u	j u

cat	Deb	Jed
cut	dam	job
cub	dud	jam
kid	did	Jill

Tom	tuff	mist	sit
sub	has	toss	sod
mast	Bob	Sam	tot
bit	fast	sum	bus
bass	set	sat	tan

Reading Chart 6

Practice saying these consonant blends.

r   g   l

a	r a	g a	l a
e	r e	g e	l e
i	r i	g i	l i
o	r o	g o	l o
u	r u	g u	l u

rug	get	lick
rob	gill	log
rib	gag	leg
red	got	lad

dill	sell	mud	till
call	jam	dam	sit
jog	cop	cuff	kiss
dug	kid	hum	hill
rag	mom	tag	did

. **125**

Reading Chart 7

Practice saying these consonant blends.

n   **w**   **p**

	n	w	p
a	na	wa	pa
e	ne	we	pe
i	ni	wi	pi
o	no	wo	po
u	nu	wu	pu

nag	well	pat
not	wit	pen
nip	wag	puff
nut	wow	pot

bet	fog	cud	Bob
Tim	den	kiss	tip
sin	mud	ham	suds
jet	mill	mitt	hat
map	hop	hot	bat

126

Reading Chart 8

v		**qu**		**y**
a	va	qua		ya
e	ve	que		ye
i	vi	qui		yi
o	vo	quo		yo
u	vu	qu		yu

Vick	quack	yam
vim	quill	yum
vat	quit	yes
vet	quest	yet

pop	wick	rub	dip
wow	God	gill	bag
will	lass	duck	top
lip	nut	lid	Jill
nest	sit	bed	mad

Reading Chart 9

Practice saying these consonant blends.

X   **Z**

	X	Z
a	ax	z a
e	ex	z e
i	ix	z i
o	ox	z o
u	ux	z u

tax	zest
fix	zip
next	Zac
fox	zot

had	van	pup	fax
yet	quiz	vet	well
rod	pin	wax	gag
vest	yes	pod	net
quill	big	wick	gig

Reading Chart 10

Practice saying these long vowel sounds.

a e i o u

ā	ay	a_e	ai
	da	ca	pa
	day	cake	paid

ē	ea	ee	ey
	be	se	ke
	bead	seed	key

ī	i_e	y	ie
	ti	fli	pi
	tide	fly	pie

ō	oe	oa	o_e	ow
	ho	so	ro	cro
	hoe	soap	rope	crow

ū	ui	u_e	ew
	su	cu	fu
	suit	cute	few

Reading Chart 11

bl	**bl**ock	gr	**gr**ass
cl	**cl**ock	pr	**pr**ay
fl	**fl**ag	tr	**tr**actor
gl	**gl**ide	sc	**sc**ale
pl	**pl**edge	sk	**sk**ate
sl	**sl**ed	sm	**sm**ell
br	**br**oom	sn	**sn**ail
cr	**cr**own	sp	**sp**ider
dr	**dr**ess	st	**st**amp
fr	**fr**y	sw	**sw**im

Reading Chart 12

dw	**dw**ell	sh	**sh**ip
squ	**squ**at	ch	**ch**urch
tw	**tw**ine	wh	**wh**ale
scr	**sc**rub	th	**th**em
			thing
spl	**spl**at		
spr	**spr**ay		
str	**str**ap		

Reading Chart 13

ll	do**ll**		lt	qui**lt**
ff	cu**ff**		mp	ju**mp**
ss	ba**ss**		nd	ba**nd**
zz	bu**zz**		ct	fa**ct**
ck	so**ck**		ft	gi**ft**
sk	de**sk**		nt	te**nt**
sp	gra**sp**		pt	we**pt**
st	ca**st**		xt	te**xt**
lf	go**lf**		ng	ri**ng**
lk	e**lk**		nk	dri**nk**
lp	he**lp**			

Reading Chart 14

ld	child	ou	hound
		ow	cow
nd	kind		
		ar	jar
gh	light		
		or	corn
ld	cold		
		$\overline{oo}$	shoot
st	post	oo	book
		u	put
th	both	o	wolf
		ou	would
ll	roll		
		oi	oil
lt	colt	oy	cowboy

Reading Chart 15

er	ve**rse**	c	**c**ity
ir	b**ir**d	g	**g**iraffe
ur	t**ur**tle	kn	**kn**ife
(w)or	**wor**ld	wr	**wr**ite
ear	**ear**th	ing	cook**ing**
		y	sk**y**
o	fr**o**g		da**y**
al	b**all**		rock**y**
aw	dr**aw**	er	work**er**
au	ha**u**l	ies	cop**ies**
augh	**caugh**t	o	M**o**ther
ough	**fough**t	a	**a**lert
		mb	li**mb**
are	b**are**	bt	dou**bt**
arr	c**arr**ot	gu	**gu**ess
air	ch**air**	bu	**bu**ild
err	b**err**y	ph	gra**ph**
ear	p**ear**	gh	lau**gh**
ere	wh**ere**		

134

Phonics Groupings

Language, in a more limited sense, is the expression of ideas by articulate sounds. In a more general sense, the word denotes all sounds by which animals express their feelings, in such a manner as to be understood by their own species.

Articulate sounds are those which are formed by the human voice, in pronouncing letters, syllables and words, and constitute the spoken language which is addressed to the ear. Letters are the marks of sounds, and the first elements of written language, which is presented to the eye.

In a perfect language, every simple sound would be expressed by a distinct character; and no character would have more than one sound. But languages are not thus perfect; and the English language is no exception.

The letters used in writing, when arranged in a certain customary order, compose what is called an *Alphabet*.

The English Alphabet consists of twenty-six letters, or single characters; and for lack of others, certain simple sounds are represented by two letters united. There are approximately forty-four different sounds in the English language.

There are two kinds of letters: *vowels* and *consonants*. A vowel is a simple articulate sound, formed without the help of another letter, by opening the mouth in a particular manner, and begun and completed with the same position of the organs. The letters which represent these sounds are **a, e, i, o, u** and sometimes **y**; but each of these characters is used to express two or more sounds.

A makes the sound of late, father, hat, care, ball, what.
E in meet, met.
I in find, pit.
O in note, not, move, dog.
U in truth, but, bush.
Y in sky, rocky.

A consonant is a letter which has no sound, or an imperfect one, without the help of a vowel. The consonants which are entirely silent, interrupt the voice by closing the organs. The hard consonants are **b, d** and **g**. The mute consonants are **k, p** and **t**.

The consonants which do not entirely interrupt all sound by closing the organs are **f, l, m, n, r, s, v,** and **z**. These are called half vowels or semi-vowels.

B has but one sound, as in bite.
C is always sounded like **k** or **s**. Like **k** when followed by **a, o** and **u**. Like **s** when followed by **e, i** and **y**.
D has only one sound, as in dress and bold.
F has its own proper sound, as in life and fever, except in of, where it has the sound of **v**.
G before **a, o** and **u**, has a hard sound, as in gun. Before **e, i** and **y** it has the same hard sound in some words, but in others it has the sound of **j**.

136

H can hardly be said to have any sound, but it denotes an aspiration or impulse of breath, which modifies the sound of the following vowel, as in **h**eart and **h**eave.

J is the mark of a compound sound or union of sounds, which may be represented by **dzh**, or the soft **g**, as in **j**elly.

K has but one sound, as in **k**ing; and before **n** is always silent, as in **k**now.

L has but one sound, as in **l**ame. It is silent before **k**, as in wal**k**.

M has but one sound, as in **m**an.

N has but one sound, as in **n**ot; and is silent after **m**, as in hym**n**.

P has one uniform sound, as in **p**it.

Q has the power of **k**, and is always followed by **u**, as in **qu**estion.

R has one sound only, as in bar**r**el.

S has the sound of **c** as in **s**o; or **z**, as in ro**s**e. When followed by **i** preceding a vowel, the syllable has the sound of **sh**, as in mi**ss**ion; or **zh**, as in o**s**ier.

T has its proper sound, as in **t**urn, at the beginning of words and end of syllables. In all terminations in **t**ion, and **t**ial, it has the sound of **sh**, as in na**t**ion, except when preceded by **s** or **x**, in which cases it has the sound of **ch** as in ques**t**ion.

V has uniformly one sound, as in **v**oice and li**v**e, and is never silent.

W has the power of a vowel, as in d**w**ell; or a consonant as in **w**ell and **w**ill.

X has the sound of **ks**, as in wa**x**; or of **gz**, as in e**x**ist, and in other words, when followed by an accented syllable beginning with a vowel. In the beginning of some words, it has the sound of **z** as in **X**erox.

Y is a vowel, as in vanit**y**, a diphthong, as in def**y**; or a consonant, as in **y**oung.

Z has its own sound usually, as in **z**eal and free**z**e.

Noah Webster's Reading Handbook can be used at any grade level as a guide or refresher for the basic phonics skills, an introduction to phonics rules and principles, or as the primary tool used to teach someone how to read.